CW00751400

Sodom, Gomorrah and the New Jerusalem:

Labour and lesbian and gay rights, from Edward Carpenter to today

by Peter Purton

With a foreword by Chris Smith

Labour Campaign for Lesbian and Gay Rights

© Peter Purton and the Labour Campaign for
Lesbian and Gay Rights 2006

ISBN 978-0-9513807-1-0

Designed and printed by Upstream, London
(TU) A workers' cooperative 020 7207 1560
www.upstream.coop

Published by the Labour Campaign for
Lesbian and Gay Rights

Labour Campaign for Lesbian and Gay Rights,
PO Box 306, London, N5 2SY
Email: info@lgbtlabour.org.uk
Voicemail & fax: 07092 332676

Peter Purton obtained a D.Phil in history from Oxford and has maintained his interest in the subject, including currently working on a major study of medieval sieges. He participated in many of the events described in this pamphlet. First becoming active in campaigns such as the Gay News Defence Campaign on behalf of Oxford Campaign for Homosexual Equality, he took part in the establishment of the Gay Activists Alliance, then joined the Labour Campaign for Gay Rights in 1982, becoming an officer in 1983, a position held until 2005. Since 1998, he has been the TUC's first LGBT rights officer.

Acknowledgements

The author would like to thank all those who assisted in the preparation of this history, in many cases through their direct participation, recorded in LCLGR publications since 1982. Particular thanks for their memories to Chris Richardson and John Shiers. John Gallagher was interviewed on his recollections of work inside the Labour Party in the 1970s by Simon Wright, and the latter, Katie Hanson, Craig Nelson, Dianne Hayter and others provided helpful ideas to improve the text. TUC staff assisted with material from the archives. Any remaining errors are, of course, the author's responsibility.

Special thanks to UNISON for generously helping to make publication possible.

Contents

Foreword: Rt. Hon. Lord Smith of Finsbury

 The last eight years have seen remarkable advances in the liberation and equality of lesbians and gay men. It hasn't been easy going, and from time to time it has been a struggle, but huge advances have been achieved: from an equal age of consent through to civil partnerships, from the scrapping of section 28 to the changes in immigration rules to the protection of employees in the workplace. Thinking back to the climate of opinion and law when I decided, back in 1984, to come out as an openly gay MP, the transformation has been astonishing. It has come about for one reason and one reason alone, and that is the existence of a Labour Government. But the decisions of that Government didn't happen by accident. They were worked for, campaigned for, argued for, lobbied for, and voted for within the Labour and Trade Union movement for years beforehand. This pamphlet documents that process, and provides real insight into what happened and how.

Peter Purton – who was himself at the heart of many of the battles that led eventually to success – chronicles these advances with real knowledge and intimacy. And he roots his analysis in the writings and thinking of Edward Carpenter, whose work as a pioneer of equality was so remarkable in the latter part of the nineteenth century.

Carpenter indeed provides the central principle that underpins everything: the simple, revolutionary concept that all human beings are of equal worth, not only regardless of income or class or status but regardless of sexual orientation too. The story chronicled here is essentially of how the rest of the labour movement, trailing more than a century behind Carpenter, came eventually to endorse this fundamental value, and then to set about making it a reality.

The Trade Unions played an essential role in this, and still do. Campaigners, both within the Labour Party and beyond, were crucial. And it couldn't have happened, either, without a host of brave individuals, Councillors, MPs, candidates and conference delegates who raised their voices and heads at a time when it was far from fashionable to do so. Deep down this is a tale of struggle, courage, determination, cussedness even, and of genuine achievement.

But however much we have won, we should never forget that there is still much to do. Homophobia and prejudice remain all too common. Violent attacks and abuse still happen, sometimes with appalling ferocity. Everything has not yet been achieved. We should rejoice, therefore, in the progress that has now at last been made. We should understand and consider how and why that happened. But we should also dedicate ourselves to ensuring that progress continues. This pamphlet will help us do all three.

Chris Smith

1. Introduction: Equal Rights, liberation, and Carpenter

2006 is the centenary of the establishment of the Parliamentary Labour Party. We are now into the third term of a Labour Government that has overseen a transformation in the position of lesbian, gay and bisexual people in Britain. We have arrived at a turning point in our communities' history: pretty much the completion of the agenda for legal equality. Under this Government, we have finally ended discriminatory treatment in the criminal law. We are protected against discrimination at work and against discrimination in the provision of goods and services. We have, in civil partnership, achieved practical equality with married heterosexuals.

This turnaround has not happened by chance. The opportunity was provided by a Labour Government, but the Labour Party did not adopt the equality agenda by accident. Rather, it responded to the aspirations of a whole community that had organised itself to campaign for justice. Most importantly, that community had found an essential ally in the labour movement, a still powerful social, economic and political force. That movement had itself begun with the joining together of working people in trade unions to assert their own rights, and continues to this day to press for social justice, fairness and equality.

This is the connection with Edward Carpenter. His name has all but disappeared from history. Otherwise knowledgeable socialists and trade unionists have never heard of him. Lesbian, gay, bisexual and trans activists are also unaware of his contribution. Many labour historians completely ignore him. A collection of his writings would fill several shelves, but not a single one of his works is in print today. In 1984, a first volume appeared of a modern attempt to publish his key works, but no further volumes appeared. Carpenter was an inspiration to generations of people who read him or heard him speak and were led to take up an unselfish socialist vision of a better world, a vision of an equal society. His impact was also felt across the world, as his writings were translated into many languages. But Carpenter was no ordinary visionary, joining a list of many well-educated middle-class idealists who have seen the evil about them and argued forcefully for a better arrangement of things. Carpenter took his vision for reality, gave up his comfortable career to live among the working masses of Sheffield, and to take his message directly to working people.

There are two even stronger reasons, though, for his place in this work. Edward Carpenter lived openly in a same-sex relationship with a partner at a time when to do so might have seemed foolhardy. But his contribution went much further even than that: it was political and theoretical as well as practical. He tackled the issue of the oppression of same-sex lovers within the framework of a liberating vision of a free society, consciously a socialist society. He explored the relationship of the "morality" of his era (which damned him and his kind) to the structure of society as a whole, and presented a well-argued and passionate advocacy of a different world. In it, women would gain their rightful place as equal partners with men, of all races everywhere, married or not. Lesbians and gay men (although these words were not then in use), and all those whose difference marked them out as inferior, even unmentionable, in Victorian and Edwardian society, would also be an equal and equally respected part of this world.

That is why Edward Carpenter is still relevant today. His socialism was part of the movement that led to the creation of the Labour Party in the first place. His vision of a society in which everyone regardless of gender, race or sexuality lives and works together in harmony is one that, one hundred years on from the foundation of the Parliamentary Labour Party, and seventy seven years since Carpenter's death in1929, still remains a distant ideal.

It is a long time since the days of Edward Carpenter, and the world has changed out of all recognition, but his relentless proselytising for socialism was part of the reason for the better elements of where we are today. Many would disagree with his view on how it was all to be brought about. But his then far-sighted understanding of the connection between lesbian and gay liberation and socialism is a lesson for today's activists.

This pamphlet is an attempt to retrace the history of the relationship between lesbian and gay equality and the labour movement, to explain how we arrived at this moment in history, and also to suggest that the task remains far from complete. Because even if equality in law has been achieved, inclusion in society has not. To defeat the deep-rooted prejudices that still lead to murderous homophobic violence, to merciless bullying in school playgrounds, to discriminatory treatment in workplaces, and to many people of all ages still fearing to reveal their sexual orientation, society itself has to change.

2. The Founding of the Labour Party

Edward Carpenter was not present in person at any of the events that led to the founding of the British Labour Party, but he was a leading figure in the movement that contributed to that slow beginning of a process that quite quickly transformed British political life. The political landscape of the second half of the nineteenth century was dominated totally by two historic parties, Tory and Liberal. In the second half of the nineteenth century, the vote was denied to many men (on the basis of property qualifications), and all women.

Trade unions had been around for half a century but were fragile, small, and lacking resources. Although strengthened by the creation of the Trades Union Congress (TUC) in 1868, the unions contributing the leadership of the movement were traditional craft organisations. Their goal in life was respectability, and their initial objective was to secure reforms in the system through the agency of Gladstone's Liberal Party, not through independent working class political action.

It was 1899 when the Congress of the TUC carried a motion to instruct its parliamentary committee to meet with the socialist societies and the co-operative movement to discuss direct representation of Labour in Parliament. This conference took place on 27 February 1900, and from it came the decision to support working class candidates, standing under a Labour banner rather than as Liberal candidates. Ramsay MacDonald was elected Secretary of the Labour Representation Committee. At the next general election, in 1906, one hundred years ago this year, the LRC, with the help of a private deal with the Liberals not to oppose one another in some seats, won the modest total of 29 seats, and when these MPs met, they formed the Parliamentary Labour Party (PLP), the Labour Representation Committee then renaming itself the Labour Party.

New Unionism and Labour representation

A transformation in trade unionism and increased suffrage were the main reasons for the break with the Liberals and the creation of an independent working class party. From the 1880s, new unions based on unskilled workers developed (such as the dockers who founded today's Transport and General Workers Union) and the bosses' response to their increased militancy had been to use the courts to penalise unions for industrial action. The Taff Vale judgement of 1900 was made against the Amalgamated Society of Railway Servants and that same union moved the proposal at the TUC to create the Labour Representation Committee. The law needed to be changed, and no other party would do that. Labour must have its own voice in Parliament.

Initially, the new Labour Party's programme was very modest, calling for reforms to help union members and some limited social improvements. The LRC clearly feared it would alienate potential voters by appearing too radical or socialist. The LRC Executive had been made up of seven trade unionists and five members of socialist societies to start with, although the Social Democratic Federation (SDF), disappointed in the political direction chosen, withdrew within a year. The unions provided the numbers, and (soon after) the finances to run elections and to ensure that Labour MPs could be remunerated. The socialists had much more far-reaching ideas but did not push them very hard. However, their views would soon come to determine that Labour's fundamental beliefs would offer socialism as the alternative to capitalism altogether.

The Socialists

A small number of socialist organisations had developed in the 1880s, although none ever had many members, and their ideas later drove the new Labour Party's agenda. At its largest, the Social Democratic Federation (founded by Henry Hyndman in 1881[1]) may have had

1,000 members. In the 1890s the thoroughly middle-class Fabian Society (established by Sidney and Beatrice Webb in 1884) reached around 150. Only the Independent Labour Party set up by Keir Hardie in 1893 had significant numbers of trade union members. William Morris[2] left the SDF in 1884 and founded the Socialist League, but this came and went with little impact, not surprising since its appeal to "idealised medievalism" (Thorpe, 1997, 10) would have had little resonance beyond the comfortable parlours of its adherents. Marxism, despite the presence of its founder in the country, had negligible impact among English socialists who rejected its apparent "economic determinism", although Hyndman had borrowed without acknowledging it large sections of Karl Marx's writings, to the intense anger of the great thinker.

This sorry tale of organisational, numerical and political weakness should not be allowed to mask the achievement of these small groups in promoting a socialist vision of a better world far, far beyond their tiny numbers. Pamphlets on every conceivable subject followed one another off the presses in great numbers, newspapers such as the SDF's *Justice* carried the message beyond the meeting rooms. Street corners across the country were taken over every weekend to deliver socialist propaganda to any who would listen, and the better known names would pack out public halls hired for lectures on current social and political issues. The new generation of trade union leaders who became prominent towards the end of the century included people like Tom Mann, Ben Tillett and Will Thorne,[3] who were all influenced by socialist ideas.

Among those who became regular speakers at many public events, and who used his own resources to assist the production of socialist propaganda, was Edward Carpenter. His cash helped Hyndman to publish *Justice*, and he himself was a member of the Fabians from 1908 until his death. Carpenter had set up his own local socialist society where he lived, in Sheffield, at first as a branch of Morris's Socialist League (1886), then soon after as an independent body.

Meeting in a room above a café rented by Carpenter, the tiny society (its core membership does not seem to have exceeded twenty) attracted speakers as varied as Annie Besant[4], Kropotkin[5] and Hyndman before collapsing through lack of funds to hold on to the building. The experience made Carpenter aware of the difficult political climate in which the socialists worked, and he described in his autobiography that at the time, they did not really grasp the extent of the apathy of the masses or the strength of the resistance of the privileged. But he made the perceptive remark that although the groups waxed and waned, their ideas succeeded in spreading. He also affirmed that it was ultimately a "good thing" that the movement had not been "pocketed by one man" (*My Days and Dreams*, 126).

3. Carpenter the man and the thinker

Born in 1844 to a middle-class family, Edward Carpenter had followed at first a traditional path, studying maths at Cambridge then becoming a cleric and a college Fellow. Unhappy with this life, closeted in so many ways, however, he came across the writings of (and later visited in person) the great US poet and visionary, Walt Whitman, whose *Leaves of Grass* had the same profound effect on Carpenter as his own writings would have in their turn on his own contemporaries. Following a trip to Italy in 1873 he resolved to "throw in my lot with ... the manual workers" (*My Days and Dreams*, 79), resigned his post and his clerical orders, and eventually went to live in Sheffield.

Initially attracted to Hyndman and the Social Democratic Foundation, he soon parted company with that sectarian and dogmatic organisation. In 1884 he joined the 'Fellowship of the New Life' along with Havelock Ellis, Olive Schreiner and Henry Salt[6] but, perhaps not surprisingly given that its basis was exclusively moral and spiritual, this small group (whose members included, for one year only, Ramsay MacDonald) disappeared after a few years. His energies then went into writing and his most influential creation, *Towards Democracy*, first appeared, at his own expense, in 1881. This largely spiritual evocation of a better world would progress through several editions and several expansions, although initially sales were slow, but would soon begin to have an effect on the growing numbers drawn to it and inspired by it to take up the cause. This work, indeed, was acknowledged by many as the source of their understanding and commitment to socialism. To Havelock Ellis it was "a kind of bible", while Raymond Unwin wrote in the same commemorative volume compiled after Carpenter's death that "the present generation may not easily realise what they owe to the liberating influence of that expression which Edward Carpenter found and uttered in *Towards Democracy*" (E Beith (ed.), *Edward Carpenter: in appreciation*, 47 and 235).

Carpenter's philosophy was actually far more libertarian than traditionally socialist – or at least, socialist if that term is construed solely in an exclusively economic sense. But it was not abstract. In the words of another admirer (the industrial secretary of the National Union of Railwaymen, C T Cramp), he had no interest in party politics, but he saw his part as being to inspire rather than direct. His own life was lived among working people, and Cramp wrote that "at home, the Sheffield cutler, engineer, miner or railwayman met poet, musician or dramatist beneath his roof and were all made to feel one of a great family." "No other socialist teacher", he went on, "so well combined a knowledge both of theory and everyday working life." (*Edward Carpenter: in appreciation*, 21, 23).

Carpenter was much in demand as a speaker at public meetings, and his independence here was a great asset, as he was happy to spread his vision from any platform, regardless of which of the socialist groups had organised the event. His speeches were not only delivered to the audiences at Fabian or ILP or similar gatherings, however, and he was also to be found addressing large numbers of workers at meetings organised by trade unions, whether it was the ASRS in his own Sheffield (1907) or the striking dockers of Greenock (1910).

For Carpenter, clearly, but also for those who invited him to speak, the workers were the vital component in advancing towards the brave new world of the future, and the trade unions were the organisations that enabled those workers to come together. His role as a great educator was commemorated by the TUC when, on his eightieth birthday in August 1924, the General Council resolved to send him a manifesto signed by every member of that body. Carpenter's reply was read out to the TUC Congress (in Hull that year), and it was agreed that his letter be placed in the record of that meeting. The following month, the TUC librarian Herbert Tracey wrote a fulsome tribute to Carpenter in *Labour Magazine*, in a section on "Makers of the Labour Movement". Tracey hailed

Carpenter as an interpreter of the "deepest thoughts and aims of the democratic movement". He concluded with the statement that his ideas "though they seem to have no bearing upon the talk of wages, hours and working conditions ... and the achievements of the Labour Government", have "helped to make the Labour Movement. Its humane and generous spirit, its hatred of tyranny, its contempt for snobbery ... its belief in the good impulses of the common people ...its faith in the future, its interest in education derive in great measure from the work of Edward Carpenter .." (*The Labour Magazine*, October 1924, 243-5).

Carpenter's vision was broad, and his writings – books, pamphlets and articles in magazines and newspapers, totalling hundreds or thousands in all – touched on subjects ranging from the land question in England to the future of India (Mahatma Gandhi was among his correspondents), to cover art, science and literature. They included major works such as *Civilisation, its cause and cure* (1889), *England's Ideal* (1885) which was almost as powerful an inspiration to its many readers as *Towards Democracy*, pamphlets such as *Towards Industrial Freedom* (1917), but also included the rousing song *England Arise!* that for a long time vied with the *Red Flag* as the anthem of the socialist movement.

The oppression of women

Among his range of interests were other questions that might not on the face of it have seemed particularly relevant to working class priorities at the time, but which were, in truth, of fundamental importance. Carpenter identified the oppression of women as resulting primarily from the distortions of human life consequent upon the rule of private property, and observed how "modern civilisation" had succeeded in reducing woman to one of three types: the idle "lady", the household drudge, or the prostitute. He identified that "nothing short of large social changes, stretching beyond the sphere of women only" could bring emancipation:

woman's cause was also that of the "oppressed labourer", and vice versa. He observed that the "rise of women will mean the active participation ... in political life" and at a practical level, he was a strong advocate of women's suffrage, both in writings and on platforms (quote from *Women, and her place in a free society*, published in 1894).

Carpenter and Merrill

This same philosophy underpinned what he had to say on homosexuality, and it also related directly to how he lived his own life. Having invested his inheritance in buying a farm and cottage at Millthorpe, a few miles from Sheffield, in 1883, Carpenter set up a co-operative there and supplied his own needs, and those of his unending procession of visitors, with his own labour and, eventually, from sale of his books. In February 1898 George Merrill, who had been born in the slums, moved in with him, and they lived together as lovers and companions for the rest of their days. It is now impossible to recover exactly how this relationship was viewed by everyone who knew of it. It was certainly not kept a secret from any of the continuing stream of visitors. The novelist E M Forster wrote of how a visit to Millthorpe inspired him to write *Maurice*, and to understand his own homosexuality.[7] It does not seem for a moment to have diminished the love or respect in which he was held locally by the working people of Sheffield amongst whom he continued to promote his views. There were those who tried to damn his views through reference to his "unspeakable sin", but all his many friends immediately rallied to his defence, and isolated and "breathed slaughter against our assailants" (*My Days and Dreams*, 164).

There can be little more uplifting than this response, or more demonstrative of the openness (acceptance or toleration, it is impossible now to say) of the workers who knew Carpenter in person: because viewed objectively, the late Victorian years in England were no time to be shamelessly flaunting one's homosexuality.

Homosexuality in late Victorian Britain

Not only was homosexuality famously, according to Oscar Wilde, "the love that dare not speak its name", indeed for a long time it had no name. The first advocates of homosexual liberation lived in a world unrecognisable to modern lesbian, gay, bisexual or trans people. Unlike some neighbouring countries, Great Britain retained medieval laws outlawing various "unnatural" offences like buggery, and indeed did not abolish the death penalty for sodomy until half way through the nineteenth century, although by then it had not been invoked for many decades. Periodically, the police would carry out raids on known male brothels or established cruising areas in big cities. When those arrested turned out, as they often did, to include professional or military men of some social importance, the press would run wild on the story, the fake prudery of the journalists only succeeding in raising the level of popular fascination by using carefully veiled language to hint at the vile behaviour of which the accused had been found guilty.

Numbers of cases were not high, but prosecutions sometimes rose to a peak during periodic crackdowns, giving rise to demands for firmer action from legislators. In 1885, during one of its regular revisions of criminal justice laws, Parliament accepted an addition to the bill it was then debating that became known after its mover as the Labouchère[8] amendment. This increased the existing penalty for anyone convicted of gross indecency. Its actual judicial effect was minimal. But it satisfied public opinion that something was being done about the dreadful decadence and depravity that was then threatening to undermine British society. This depravity was not homosexuality, a word that would not have been understood by the public that avidly purchased the tabloids of the day for accounts of the trials, as it had only recently been coined by a Hungarian named Benkert (in 1869). Rather, it was any kind of sexual behaviour outside that sanctioned by church and state. But men engaging in sexual acts with other men were among the most frequent victims of the criminal law.

First challenges

However, for the first time in modern history, this condemnation of same-sex love was being challenged. The lesbian, gay, bisexual and trans movement should hold dear the memory of those who took those first and extremely brave steps, notably the first to openly proclaim from a public platform that same-sex love was natural, Karl Ulrichs (in 1869),and Magnus Hirschfeld who founded a committee to try to reform German law. The latter's notion of an "intermediate sex" influenced Carpenter's writings. However, at that time, not only was acceptance out of sight, even gaining a hearing was well nigh impossible. Instead, society put its trust in medicine and several generations of doctors (and then psychiatrists) devoted research to finding a "cure" for homosexuality. These ranged from castration to cold baths and aversion therapy, and the echoes of these parodies of science have been heard through many subsequent decades.

Carpenter's writings on homosexuality

So when Edward Carpenter, who recognised quite early in life that he was one of these "unnaturals", turned his mind to writing about the subject, he could not expect a ready audience for his own ideas. He did his research, he studied the writings of Ulrichs, of Krafft-Ebing and also used those of Walt Whitman to reach his own conclusions. For this classical scholar, the love of which he wrote was *homogenic*, and following Ulrichs and others, it was an *inversion* of the normally accepted love. Carpenter was proud to be an invert.

Carpenter pointed out that "homogenic love" had been known across all recorded history and was common in all kinds of societies up to the present day. He called on literary evidence, too, of its existence from all times. Making a firm stand for equality, he called on the scientific findings of Ulrichs and others to show that "sexual inversion is ... quite instinctive and congenital .. entwined in the very roots of individual life and practically ineradicable"; that it was numerous; and – a crucial argument - that it does not differ "from the rest of mankind or womankind." He recognised that all the evidence of history, literature and art was not sufficient to overcome humanity's prejudice against anything "a little exceptional". He noted that the science of his age always began with the same false prejudgement that "generation is the sole object of love". He observed the potential of freed homogenic love to help in the move towards the creation "of new forms of society, new orders of thought, and new institutions of human solidarity". Noting once again his understanding of the connection with women's liberation, he wrote that "in this deepest relation of politics (that) the movement among women towards their own liberation and emancipation ... has been accompanied by a marked development of the homogenic passion among the female sex." Logically, he concluded that private morals were not the province of the law. (Quotations from *Homogenic Love, and its place in a free society*).

Carpenter's first collection of writings on sex and sexuality had sold very well, up to 4,000 copies. He brought them together in a volume entitled *Love's Coming of Age* in 1895. At the same time, *Homogenic Love* was ready for publication. This was the year that the trial of Oscar Wilde had generated yet another press frenzy about sexual depravity and the collapse of morals, and all of a sudden, Carpenter found himself without a publisher. Homogenic Love appeared initially in a small edition printed by Manchester Labour Press, for private distribution only among a carefully selected audience. It was his first, but not his last writing on the subject, and he later developed the theories advanced there at greater length in another work, *The Intermediate Sex*, a substantial work in which *Homogenic Love* was included, in 1908. This time, with the hysteria that followed the Wilde trial already history, there was no public or press furore. The little book was reprinted a number of times, making a significant contribution to a debate that was at last beginning to make some progress during the first years of the twentieth century. Carpenter was to be one of the main instigators of the foundation of the British

Society for the Study of Sex Psychology, following a lecture by Hirschfeldt at an international gathering, in 1913. But the progress would be drastically interrupted by the First World War and the political, economic and social upheavals that accompanied and followed it.

There are many weaknesses in Carpenter's theory and much that to the modern mind is pure fantasy in his solution. But nor should modern readers fail to recognise in it the true voice of liberation – not just liberation for those of a different sexuality, but liberation for all in which a new society will transcend the barriers of the old. He argues that oppression should end because it is wrong, sexual inversion is both natural, and normal. More than that, by being allowed their natural place in human life, "inverts" could contribute to transforming society for the better. He located these ideas in his general theories of humanity and society, tying this in with his socialist vision. In the process he offered a way of making socialism itself not just a stronger creed, but a more vibrant and encompassing way of life. This was truly revolutionary for its day, and the vision is all too easily lost sight of in the detail of day to day political struggle.

4. From Ramsay MacDonald to Harold Wilson

The newly created Labour Party was far from ready to take on (or even listen to) such views. The modesty of its first manifesto has already been mentioned, and the course of subsequent external developments left little room or opportunity to advance much in the way of anything *socially* radical. In truth, for all the successes achieved by socialist propagandists in extending the reach of their ideas, the hard-headed trade union leaders who were the predominant influence on party policy were unlikely to look beyond calling for immediate economic reforms designed to benefit workers on a limited range of issues. Labour *did* support extending the electoral franchise to women voters, and indeed benefited considerably from votes from newly enfranchised women in the 1918 election, but apart from the vote, other steps to change the position of women were not yet on the agenda. Rather, a male-dominated trade union movement continued to believe that women's place was in the home, and man's on the shop floor, and had resisted proposals to call for child benefit and family allowance in case this led to a reduction in (male) workers' wages.

The socialism that the Party did adopt, in its much more far-reaching 1918 programme *Labour and the New Social Order*, was still restricted to retaining control by the state of the sectors taken over during the First World War, such as rail and mining. This is not to downplay the importance of the demands themselves. Other social demands covered better education and more welfare. Similar themes – benefits, education and council housing – not surprisingly dominated the practical activity of the short-lived first Labour government in 1924, its room for manoeuvre anyway constrained by its being a minority dependent on Liberal votes.

After losing office, the Party's overall programme was focussed on a policy to overcome the grotesque injustices caused by capitalism. It planned to do so by parliamentary means, nationalising land, the railways and energy (particularly mining), improving the position of the unemployed and unfettering trade unions from the hostile restrictions legislated by the Tories. This was the gist of the programme agreed at the 1928 conference. In its published form, women were mentioned in just three paragraphs in 44 pages, in the context of increased spending on social security (*Labour and the Nation*, 1927 and 1928). The 1937 party programme was little different, adding a massive programme of public works to deal with unemployment blackspots. Alongside this official party material, the ILP continued to publish numerous pamphlets explaining socialism to the masses. Not even women get a mention (*ILP: The Socialist Programme*, 1923; Fred Henderson, *The ABC of Socialism*, 1924).

Sadly therefore, the idea that any of the political parties at this time would take up the most pressing first step towards equal treatment for homosexuals (or indeed for racial or other minorities), is fanciful. No political leader would risk suggesting even reform of the law, and probably none of them actually believed it was a good idea anyway. No such argument was advanced from within mainstream politics.

The 1930s appear to have seen some lessening of social intolerance compared with Victorian times with a vibrant sub-culture in many cities and increasing representations in literature and art. The sexologists' classification of "the homosexual" started to appear in popular culture, some of which argued weakly against criminal persecution. However, strict conformity returned with a vengeance during the years of austerity and cold war witch hunts that followed the Second World War. The hidden homosexual subculture remained vulnerable to raids by the police, whose ardour for prosecuting same-sex lovers, in fact, seems to have continued unabated until the last few years of the twentieth century. The trade unions, too, not only had other priorities, but also shared many conservative social attitudes with their contemporaries. The eulogy of Carpenter by Herbert Tracey already quoted refers to his "bachelor house" and to his working the farm with his "friends", which may have served as coded references to his homosexuality. But they would probably have been lost on most of the readers: nothing more was said about his partner or his publications on the intermediate sex, although it is inconceivable that Tracey was unaware of them.

If the writings of Carpenter and his fellow sexual radicals had raised hopes of change in a new era, these soon disappeared. No one would carry the torch for several decades, and the labour movement remained silent and complicit. In this story, the whole period through to the end of Attlee's Labour government in 1951 must be passed over as a desert. Perhaps strangely, the first significant developments would actually begin during the Conservative administration that then took office.

Scandals and blackmail

Not for the first time, attention to the state of the criminal law would be brought about as a result of the activities of the police. During the whole of the period 1935-39, there had been 299 reported offences of indecency between males in Britain. In 1952 alone, there were 1,686, and the number continued to rise year on year, with a high percentage being sent to prison. It was when people of rank were involved that newspapers and politicians began to take notice, and this happened in 1953 with the prosecutions of an MP (Labour's William Field), an author, the actor John Gielgud, and (twice) the peer Lord Montagu of Beaulieu. (Figures from Jeffrey-Poulter, *Peers, Queers and Commons*.) At the end of the year, two MPs, one Tory and one Labour, called for a royal commission to review the law, a move initially rejected by the Home Secretary. The first ever House of Commons debate on homosexuality took place in May 1954, and with an election near, and wanting to shelve the subject for as long as possible, the Government agreed to appoint a commission to examine the law on prostitution and homosexuality. It asked Lord Wolfenden, vice-chancellor of Reading University, to chair it.

Wolfenden Report

Wolfenden finally reported in September 1957 and his proposals challenged the very basis of existing law - but they also maintained the inferior status of homosexual men, and, by extension of the thinking behind, if not the word of, the law, lesbians too. He recommended that all forms of consensual sex between men, in private, be made legal, but with an age of consent of 21, a fudge arrived at in order to reach consensus on his committee. So for the second time, MPs were faced with dealing with the issue, and did so in a debate on the report in November 1957, during which all the old prejudices were wheeled out, and were rehearsed for frequent repetition for the coming forty years. Although there was support for enacting the recommendations, chiefly from the Liberal and Labour benches, there was no majority to do so, and the Conservative Home Secretary, Rab Butler,[9] refused to do anything.

Wolfenden's report was now parked, and it would have to wait another ten years until a Labour Government made action on it possible. Meanwhile, however, for the first time, the people who had not so far been invited to the party began to make themselves heard. A new organisation with both homosexual and straight members, the Homosexual Law Reform Society (HLRS) was founded, and in 1960 it nervously organised the first-ever public meeting on the subject of homosexual law reform in London. It was a great success, and carried a motion calling for the implementation of Wolfenden. Encouraged and lobbied by the HLRS, Labour MPs now, for the first time, took up the issue, and one MP, Kenneth Robinson,[10] presented a private member's bill to enact the recommendations. It was crushingly defeated in the vote, with the Tories marshalled against it by Butler again, but attracted strong backing from Labour benches where Roy Jenkins, Richard Crossman and Tony Greenwood all spoke in its support. Prominent Labour parliamentarians were now willing to speak out in public in support of law reform, which boded well for when the Party finally succeeded in ousting the long-lived Tory regime.

This shift did not take place in a vacuum. Various elements combined to contribute to an improvement in social attitudes. At Government level, there was deepened concern over the threat of blackmail that the existing law clearly encouraged. This had first made headlines with the 1951 defection of the spies Burgess and Maclean to the Soviet Union at the height of the cold war, following their being threatened with blackmail. In 1962, William Vassall, a Foreign Office clerk in Moscow, was sensationally prosecuted for selling secrets to the Soviets - he had been blackmailed by the KGB, who had information about his homosexuality. It attracted much public attention and led directly to calls for enacting Wolfenden. Alongside these negative pressures, a positive case for law reform was being articulated in films such as *Victim* (1961) starring one of Britain's biggest film stars, Dirk Bogarde. The combination of new developments – the blackmail issue, greater public awareness and more open debate, and the voice of homosexual men and women making itself heard for the first time – established a new reality from which the Labour Government of Harold Wilson that took office in 1964 might find the strength to act.

The 1967 Act

Wilson's first two governments (his majority, being just four in 1964, required him to call another election in 1966 which increased it to nearly a hundred) were the first to oversee serious legal reform in the social arena. It is to the Parliament of that time that we owe not only the legalisation of abortion, but also the putting into effect of Wolfenden's recommendations. But it is important to notice that none of this legislation was introduced by the Government itself. The Prime Minister was unwilling to take that step. Instead, Wilson relied on backbench MPs bringing forward the bills, which his parliamentary managers then offered to assist to enable them to progress. Thus, support was offered, but the initiative had to remain elsewhere. However, the strength of opposition from Tory MPs, no doubt representing the views and prejudices of many of those they represented, shows clearly that it was only with a Labour government that any progressive reform could have been achieved.

In July 1966, Leo Abse (Labour MP for Pontypool) introduced a bill to legislate Wolfenden's recommendations which obtained a large majority on first reading. Crucially, Abse, Roy Jenkins and Richard Crossman then persuaded Wilson to allow it space in the parliamentary timetable, and the Sexual Offences Bill completed its parliamentary progress after an all-night sitting in July 1967. It had not come through its stages unscathed. Male homosexuality was now legal, providing it was between not more than two persons, in private, did not extend to the armed forces or merchant navy, and was not effective in Scotland or Northern Ireland. The range of acts that were still criminal was actually extended to include procurement.

Predictably, perhaps, the effects of the 1967 Act were contradictory. The interpretation of the wording on privacy actually opened up new opportunities for the police to raid clubs, and police activity against gay men actually increased after the enactment of the law.

Most politicians however believed that the issue was now dealt with, and might quietly be put to one side. Lord Arran, speaking in the Lords, stated that victory had been won for Oscar Wilde's cause, and "today sees the end of that road" (quoted in Jeffery-Poulter, 81). In this they were, of course, seriously disappointed. The next stages in the battle for equality would be characterised by a rather different set of players to any of those who had brought about the enactment of Wolfenden. For the first time, an open movement of lesbians and gay men would raise the stakes in the debate, push out the agenda far beyond the scope of the criminal law, and make possible future advances. For the first time too, the labour movement would align itself with these demands, and make their achievement possible. But not just yet!

5. The Lesbian and Gay Movement and the Labour Government 1974-79

The Homosexual Law Reform Society had played an important part in bringing about the 1967 Act, and it continued to function while changing its focus. One effect was to see its transformation into the Campaign for Homosexual Equality (CHE) in 1970. It would continue to carry out significant work, pressing for further improvements to the legal position and in lobbying ministers, although even any possibility of success had to await the coming, and going, of Heath's Conservative government (1970-74), brought down in the end by a powerful trade union movement.

Gay Liberation Front

Meanwhile another exciting development had occurred that would have its own dramatic impact on the movement for lesbian and gay rights in Britain. In June 1969, the Stonewall riots in New York had led to the creation of the Gay Liberation Front (GLF), and in November 1970, its British equivalent was launched following a meeting of activists who wanted something far more radical than what they perceived as CHE's polite lobbying. The first London Gay Pride march took place on 1 July 1972, and the first edition of a campaigning newspaper, *Gay News*, was published at the same time. No longer would those who made up the GLF cower in hiding, live in an underworld of coded language and fear of police entrapment, no longer would they seek to pass as straight in public. The old ways were to be banished, Gay was good.

By the early 1970s, therefore, a public movement of lesbians and gay men existed in Britain for the first time, and in the nature of such things, it already had two wings that operated in very different ways, although overlap did happen – a division of approach that has continued in various organisational forms to the present day. Now, again for the first time, there were visible lesbian and gay communities.

Nonetheless, for the time being at least, the absence of almost any legal rights whatever, and the widespread discrimination against lesbians and gay men in every sphere of life, meant that any long-term changes for the community had to be based on changing these conditions. Deliberately without leaders, structure or immediate political objectives, GLF inevitably failed to last very long as an organisation. Its importance lay in the impact it had on the world view of the many lesbians and (more numerous) gay men who either took part, or else (the majority) were inspired by its example.

Their vision of liberation from oppression was often contrasted at the time with the seemingly timid pleading of CHE to be granted rights by the establishment, although in truth such a distinction was artificial and unhelpful. Nonetheless, supporters of the CHE approach over the years would be found condemning the "in your face" stunts and public activities of liberationists as counterproductive, and leading to the alienation of the very same people whose support was needed if further reform was to be achieved. As with all such movements, after the peak of activity there came a very rapid trough, with numbers reduced to the core of the most committed activists while most supporters moved on to other things. That core would continue to work through a variety of campaigning organisations throughout the 1970s, although without much apparent success.

Male domination of the movement

A similar affliction would also weaken CHE, in this case hastened by a difference amongst its members about pursuing law reform, or investing energy instead in becoming a support and social group to assist the development of a community network. Both CHE and GLF and its descendants suffered as well from a more or less complete failure – in practice - to recognise that lesbians were oppressed too, as lesbians, not just as a subset of gay men. It should have been no surprise that many lesbian campaigners seemed to prefer to work alongside their straight sisters in the organisations of the women's liberation movement. In CHE, focussed mainly on reform of a criminal law designed specifically to benefit gay men, rather than dealing with the widespread discrimination faced by lesbians as lesbians in many other areas of the law, such disenchantment was no surprise.

In GLF, lesbians faced rather a total lack of comprehension of what they were arguing. It would be quite some time before the gender balance of lesbian and gay organisations began to improve so that they reflected the communities in reality rather than simply in name. Indeed, it was some time before many campaign groups recognised, firstly, that to call themselves "gay" did not include lesbians; and secondly, that just changing their name did *not* suddenly render them inclusive, but that they needed to broaden their objectives, structures and ways of working.

It is worth noting that similar battles had to be fought and won for the inclusion of bisexuals within the movement (an issue not resolved until the 1990s). Meanwhile, trans people, who had been active participants in the early gay liberation movement, found themselves outside, and were compelled to work alone, until eventually winning inclusion in the movement even later.[11]

Wilson-Callaghan Government

For those who did focus on law reform, the return of the Labour Party to government in 1974 after four years of Tory rule seemed to offer good prospects for success. CHE had drawn up a draft bill to equalise the legal standing of lesbians and gay men, which it pressed the new Government to adopt. The signs were hopeful, and, continuing the trend developing during the debates around the 1967 law, there was widespread support among Labour MPs for further reform. Home Secretary Roy Jenkins asked the Criminal Law Revision Committee to investigate, and a report was made in 1975 encouraging the removal of various inequalities that remained in the 1967 Act. Lord Arran presented proposals to the House of Lords in

1977 that would reduce the age of consent, albeit only to 18, but that is where the progress came to a halt. Their Lordships overwhelmingly threw out Arran's measure. The same year, the editor of *Gay News*, Denis Lemon, was prosecuted in the courts for the truly anachronistic offence of blasphemous libel, and found guilty.

Reactionary backlash

Both events owed much to the workings of a new coalition of religious fundamentalists, the Festival of Light, fronted by the charismatic bigot Mary Whitehouse. The newspapers lapped it all up: this was the righteous backlash of the "silent majority" against the ever more pressing demands of gay liberationists to have the right to corrupt British youth. Vigorously lobbied by the FOL, the House of Lords had witnessed a strong turnout of the backwoodsmen and women rallying to the defence of family values, decency and wholesomeness and a repetition of the same arguments raised against Wolfenden two decades before. In the climate of widespread intolerance that now swept the media, and given the strength of the vote in the Lords, the Government withdrew into its shell. When Maureen Colquhoun (Labour) was outed as the first openly lesbian MP that same year, she received no public backing from the party leadership. Instead, and shamefully, she was not reselected at least in part due to her being identified as a lesbian.

In 1978, gay stories continued to claim the attention of the tabloids with the sensational trial of the leader of the Liberal Party, Jeremy Thorpe, for conspiring to murder a male model. Those who were involved at the time remember the late 70s as a time of attack after attack. They continued the work of arguing for equal rights, organised significant demonstrations that attracted thousands of lesbians and gay men into the streets (as in the demonstration organised by the National Gay News Defence Campaign in 1978). They continued to organise annual Pride marches. But they were fighting to hold on to their right to be heard, no longer pressing for further legal reform, let alone liberation. They were back on the defensive.

When Labour Prime Minister Callaghan went to the polls in 1979, those in the movement for lesbian and gay liberation had little enough cause to thank Labour, either in government or in the trade union movement, for their backing during the previous decade.

But the work that had been done in the years since the 1967 Act to bring the cause of equality before the eyes of the public had not been done in isolation. Other important developments had taken place. Not for the first or the last time, women had shown the way. The Wilson-Callaghan government had been responsible for the Sex Discrimination Act (1975), and had also adopted a positive approach to dealing with a growing awareness of the problem of racism against ethnic minority communities with the Race Relations Act. The sexism of the trade unions that had limited the demands of the Labour Party in its early years had now been transformed into positive support for women's equality. The labour movement had woken up to the fact that discrimination against half the population was not in its interest. It had been made aware that (despite, or perhaps because of, the initially reactionary response of some sections of its own membership), racial discrimination was not only

bad in itself, but divisive and destructive of its own unity. Better terms and conditions and higher wages naturally remained at the heart of trade unionism. But during the 1970s, unions were brought to understand that trade unionism, if it was to be truly effective, must involve more than this.

By opening the door to a better understanding of their role in society, women had also prepared the way for others to show that discrimination and injustice weakened the whole of the labour movement cause. Inside the Party, a similar process was underway as Labour's Women's Sections began to assert their right to discuss policy, not just make the tea. In fact, some homosexuals were to explore the possibility of calling on the Sex Discrimination Act to protect them against discrimination on the grounds of their sexuality rather than their sex, but this route was to prove a dead end, the cases failing. But in broader terms, the cause of lesbian and gay rights was significantly helped by the challenge successfully made by women to the prevailing narrow horizons of the labour movement.

Organisation inside the Labour Party:
Gay Labour and LCGR

The emergence of an open movement of lesbians and gay men campaigning for their own rights had also found its reflection among members of the Labour Party. One of the founding members, John Gallagher remembers debates on gay rights at conferences of the Young Socialists as early as 1972. Notably, the adoption of policy was rejected by the Militant group then dominant within the Young Socialists. After the 1974 election, Gallagher and others got together and decided to put an advertisement in the gay press inviting Labour party members to a meeting to form a "gay labour caucus". They met formally for the first time at the CHE office in 1975. The Gay Labour Group then began to hold regular meetings attracting some 20-30 activists, as well as annual away weekends

In 1975, the first Gay Labour group fringe meeting was held at Labour's annual conference – a tradition that appears to have continued unbroken to the present day. They also began to hold regular discos at conference which led to battles with the Party machinery if it tried not to advertise these fully. The Gay Labour Group also began a tradition of taking its banner on any marches – ensuring that the wider Labour movement saw that the gay rights agenda was considered a worthy and equal struggle to other, more traditional, labour demands. Another early member of the Gay Labour group was an Islington councillor, Chris Smith, before he became a Member of Parliament. From the start, the group related very closely to CHE's campaign agenda. At the 1978 AGM, held in Camden, the Group changed its name to Labour Campaign for Gay Rights (LCGR). In 1979, it had around 50 members, and had begun to have discussions with supportive MPs and with Party officers on issues such as policing, and employment rights.

With the coming to power of Margaret Thatcher in the 1979 election, and then again in 1983 and 1987, followed by John Major's election victory of 1992, a long period of social reaction set in, deliberately cultivated by the Tories and ably promoted by sections of the press. The prospects for achieving anything in the way of reform, let along positive social change, were rightly recognised as gloomy, and indeed defensive actions were needed far more often than any progressive move. But these years were also to witness the critical advances within the labour movement that would make possible the triumphant changes that have now occurred. They had been a long time coming, and each step of the way they had to be protected against attempts at backsliding from the Labour Party leadership, as will be shown, but the goal was eventually achieved and the ground prepared for fundamental changes.

6. 1979-1997:
Winning the Labour Movement

The downfall of the Callaghan government, and in particular the failure of its economic policies that had led to the critical confrontation in 1978/9 with public sector and especially local government unions that had occasioned its fall, led to a drastic rethink about policy and direction for Labour. A strong left wing led by MPs such as Tony Benn quickly took the lead, criticising the whole approach previously adopted and calling for Labour to return to the socialist policies of its roots. But this was not just a return to the economic socialism of the first years, it was also a socialism for the modern age that took on board the social issues that had come to the fore during the previous decade or so. Among the consequences was that large numbers of left wing activists, generally much more open to accepting the arguments for equality, now joined the Party, in many cases taking over moribund branches and constituency parties. A new wave of lesbian and gay campaigners themselves followed the same approach, and provided one of the crucial components of the alliance that would ultimately transform the Party's policy.

LCGR in new hands

Activists had been working in the Manchester Labour Party to win inclusion of lesbian and gay equality in the city council's agenda. Local events, including problems with getting the Labour Club to host gay discos, and a campaign to defend a local Labour MP arrested for cottaging, persuaded John Shiers, David Mottram, Paul Fairweather and others of the need to link up with similar developments elsewhere and to create a national network. The existence of the Labour Campaign for Gay Rights (LCGR) provided a platform to work from. Its approach of quiet internal lobbying was not the way forward wanted by the new generation. The members from Manchester, along with people from Nottingham such as Chris Richardson, and many others who had worked together through the various campaigns of the 1970s resolved to make a change of strategic direction, and to take advantage of the ferment in Labour to win it to an active campaigning stance for lesbian and gay equality. Progress in local government and the publication by Labour's National Executive Committee of the *Rights of Gay Men and Women* (see below) provided the impetus. LCGR provided the existing vehicle, and at a special meeting in Manchester of some 50 campaigners in June 1981 it was transformed.

The change of direction and strategy was consolidated by an AGM held in Nottingham in July 1982 that confirmed the break with the previous leaders of the group and agreed a new constitution, and set of aims and adopted a loose regional structure with quarterly national gatherings to agree policy and action. Groups were formed where support was strong, which was particularly in the East Midlands, Manchester, Bristol, and London, to work inside Labour for the agreed aims. Within a couple of years, lesbians had secured the

Some of the campaigners who took part in the LCGR AGM in Nottingham, July 1982. Despite appearances, there were actually a few lesbian activists present at the meeting. Photo kindly supplied by Chris Richardson.

addition of their name to its title and thenceforward always made up a vital component of what was now LCLGR's active membership. Another important decision was that the Campaign should be active across the whole of the labour movement.

Although total numbers were small – never more than a few hundred - the impact would be substantial, as the climate was favourable to listening to, and taking on, new demands and issues. In truth, what this represented was not just some individual campaigners joining in with the political battles inside Labour, it was part of the *liberation movement* deciding that Labour was the surest way to bring about the desired results. No one at the time believed it would turn out to be quite so hard to win inside the Party. No one thought that Labour would lose quite so many consecutive elections. Many of those who had taken part at the beginning dropped out or focussed on other work as the years and conferences and internal disputes rolled by. But sufficient remained committed to the project, along with a change in the constitution to replace the open quarterly meetings with an elected committee, to prevent LCLGR disappearing the same way as many other small campaigning organisations.

LCLGR was vital but it was only part of the reason for the coming victories. If LCLGR was critical in leading the argument for party policy, it was reliant on those outside its ranks for spreading the word and winning the votes. From the beginning, the group allied itself with others striving for Labour's support, striking up working relations for example with members campaigning for black sections, and supporting the work of disabled lesbians and gay men to establish their own voice. Studiously and deliberately avoiding becoming part of any of the left wing currents then flourishing within the Party, despite the personal views of most leading activists, LCLGR succeeded in attracting the positive backing of many prominent MPs. But the critical weight required to win was provided by the unions.

Lesbian and gay trade union groups

The same lesbian and gay activists who were joining the Labour Party were also active in their trade unions, alongside other activists who had been working to persuade these organisations to take up the rights of their lesbian and gay members. Public sector trade unions were particularly well advanced in responding to the pressure, but many unions were heading in the same direction. At this point, however, the movement towards recognising lesbian and gay members' groups within trade unions themselves was only slowly developing. Surveys carried out by CHE in 1981 (published as *What about the Gay Workers?*), and then by LAGER (Lesbian and Gay Employment Rights) in 1985/6 showed however that there was a dramatic increase over these few years both in the number of trade unions with organised groups of lesbian and gay members, and the number of unions that had actually adopted lesbian and gay equality policies. The formal adoption of policy, in many cases, represented the official step after the fact of actual recognition. The long list of unions adopting policies included giant general unions such as the Transport and General Workers, alongside large public sector unions and smaller specialist and sectoral organisations. Sometimes the initiative came from the top, but very often it came from members organising at a local level and winning the support of union leaderships, or securing conference debates and votes.

Employment cases

There had been a number of cases during the 1970s when members being victimised by the employer for being lesbian or gay had not received support from their unions, alongside others where such support had been forthcoming at either a local or national level. But these matters had generally attracted little outside notice. In a case that did gain national attention, John Saunders was sacked by his employers (who ran a Scottish residential children's camp) for no reason other than that he was gay, and the industrial tribunal and the appeal courts backed the decision. The sacking took place in 1979, the hearings in 1980, and the tale highlighted the vulnerability of lesbians and gay men in the workplace. There was much anger at this ruling, and prominent celebrities joined in a petition launched by the Scottish Minorities Group (the equivalent to CHE), the National Council for Civil Liberties (NCCL – now Liberty), and others calling for laws to end such discrimination. Many trade union leaders added their names to the petition, and many trade unionists saw the need for their organisations to give proper backing to members who found themselves so disgracefully treated. Those working with children or young people, or with anyone seen as "vulnerable", were exceptionally at risk from ignorant and prejudiced employers, and it is not surprising that unions organising among such workers were early among those recognising the problem. The same arguments about predatory homosexuals corrupting youth that had been used to justify continued criminalisation and an unequal age of consent were now given judicial sanction in employment law too.

Saunders had not been a union member, but Susan Shell was. She was sacked from her job as a care assistant at a residential home by the London Borough of Barking in May 1981 on revealing her sexuality in conversation. She was a member of NUPE (the National Union of Public Employees) and had that union's full support, but had no legal recourse to challenge her directly discriminatory dismissal. Only a change in the law would bring such an improvement, and only Labour was likely to deliver such a change, if first it could be convinced of the need to do so. NUPE became the first trade union to affiliate itself at a national level to LCLGR, in 1984. It was also one of the three large public sector unions that later came together to form UNISON (the others were local government union NALGO and health workers' union COHSE), and this has been the union with the most advanced structures and policies in this area to the present day.

The involvement of the unions in the campaign for legal equality was not only vital to its success, it was also vital in widening out the perception and understanding of the areas of law that required attention from the criminal law, that had been the main focus since Wolfenden, to *all* discriminatory laws.

Events moved rapidly. The European Court ruled in favour of Jeff Dudgeon, a citizen of Northern Ireland, requiring that the Tory government ensure that the 1967 Act apply in that place (at last). Tony Benn publicly called for Labour to back lesbian and gay equality in 1981. In March, the Party's National Executive Committee published *The Rights of Gay Men and Women* as a discussion document. This was dynamite: not only was it the first official party document to raise the question, it also unequivocally called for equality. The General Secretary, Ron Hayward, introduced it with the explicit statement:

> *As socialists we cannot be concerned about inequalities of class, wealth and privilege and ignore the inequalities experienced by minorities such as homosexuals. The elimination of prejudice and injustice in our society is fundamental to the fight for socialism.*

The text of the document, based on CHE's draft bill, focussed initially on the deficiencies of the 1967 Act, but moved on to raise the issue of employment discrimination with a direct reference to the *Saunders* and other cases, and a listing of the kinds of services that were allowed to discriminate at will. Although it was only a discussion paper, rather than any kind of policy, the pro-Tory press sprang on it as if it was the chance they had been waiting for to smear Labour as pro-gay. But the support continued to mount regardless. Ken Livingstone, Labour leader of the Greater London Council, delivered a speech promising to give backing to lesbian and gay equality in the capital, that received wide press coverage that same year. It would be in local government, wherever Labour ran the council, that immediate steps could be taken to assist in the equality arena, with such steps as offering funding to lesbian and gay groups, helplines and so on. Each decision to do so raised a press uproar about ratepayers' money being spent on a deviant minority, conveniently ignoring the reality that the beneficiaries were also ratepayers, and had previously received nothing in return!

Bermondsey 1983, Gay's The Word 1984

The press onslaught was relentless, and came to a fearsome peak in the parliamentary by-election in Bermondsey (February 1983). The target was the local Labour candidate, known gay left wing activist Peter Tatchell, who was challenged by the deselected previous MP, Bob Mellish. During weeks of campaigning, homophobic bigotry appeared to rule the day on the doorstep, with Tatchell's homosexuality becoming central to the attacks on Michael Foot's Labour Party. The seat was won by the Liberals, with many Labour activists blaming them for running a homophobic campaign to take control of working class Bermondsey. The sheer venom of the anti-gay campaign was breathtaking, all the more ironic since the later outing of the Liberal victor Simon Hughes. The first public signs of confusion on the Labour front bench were also becoming apparent. It certainly did not help Tatchell that when challenged about the views of the candidate on extra-parliamentary action in the Commons, the Party leader Michael Foot disowned him. The following year (April 1984) there began what turned into its own remarkable saga when HM Customs and Excise raided the community bookshop Gay's The Word in London, and brought a scroll-full of criminal charges against the directors for importing literature that included material that had been published and was freely available already in Britain. Yet another defence campaign had to be organised and run by the community, and was.

The promotion of lesbian and gay equality continued, however, despite the rampant hostility and the obvious rejection by Thatcher's government of anything that might advance equality. Another strong supporter, Labour MP Jo Richardson, introduced her Sex Equality bill in the House in 1983. Not surprisingly, it was lost. But it had been important in promising to outlaw discrimination in employment on grounds of sexual orientation.

Local Government advances

The work continued in local government as well, with Labour councils under progressive leadership increasingly recognising the lead of London, Manchester and other big cities, and offering support to lesbian and gay groups. In many cases, the first step involved getting councils to extend their existing equal opportunities policies to encompass sexuality, which would provide the platform from which all the local authority's policies could be examined, and amended accordingly. In London, a Lesbian and Gay Working Party was established to begin this task and to act as a consultation forum for the community in the capital.

Rugby 1984

To the reactionaries, it seemed like gay propaganda was washing over the whole country in a flood, carrying the threat of corruption with it. When the midlands town of Rugby under a combative right wing council leader refused a call from Labour councillors to extend its equal opportunities policy in this way, the *Sun* gave it front page headlines and praised at as a "brave little town" standing up to the tide of evil, and defending traditional family values. A counter-campaign was organised. LCGR (as it was still) helped to mobilise for a demonstration that took place in Rugby on 10 November 1984. At the rally that concluded the march, Chris Smith, elected in 1983 as MP for Islington South and Finsbury, one of the guest speakers, came out publicly as gay to a prolonged standing ovation from everyone present. The press response was less warm, but also rather more measured than might have been expected. To many, this first voluntary coming out of a gay Labour MP was a turning point in the continuing campaign to ensure that Labour would stand firmly for equality.

AIDS

Meanwhile, to add to the constant media interest, this time also saw the first recognition in Britain of the arrival of the still little-understood HIV virus, and the first deaths from AIDS-related conditions. Once again, the tabloids swung into action, and "gay plague" headlines raised the temperature still further. This was not, of course, a very productive way of dealing with a new disease. The community itself began to do something about it, however, with the setting up of support and information groups like the Terrence Higgins Trust, and many unions, that began over the next few years to publish and distribute advice on AIDS to their members and shop stewards. The government's own response was constrained by its initial refusal to talk publicly about sex, or at least gay sex, as a transmission route for HIV. In consequence its eventual advertising campaign generated much panic but spread little serious information on how the virus could be transmitted. It was no surprise to find that discrimination against both lesbians and gay men (despite the absurdity of including lesbian women in the frame) increased further as a result of popular ignorance, for which the press, and even more the government, bore a heavy responsibility.

Inside Labour: Blackpool fringe 1982

Campaigners were making things happen in the only arena in which Labour held some power, local government, but in a national climate where reaction reigned and the prospect of legal equality was at least as far distant as the next general election. Nor was it unnoticed that the Party itself still, actually, had no official policy on reforming existing discriminatory laws, let alone introducing new measures such as those needed to end discrimination. The NEC discussion paper raised hopes that this could be changed, but since its publication it had run into opposition: Benn, Joan Lestor and Jo Richardson among others had tried to get a commitment to it into the 1982 party programme but had been voted down. The newly reformed LCGR turned to trying to overcome the lack of policy through pressing for inclusion in the progressive agenda at Labour's annual conference, although the impetus was in a very unexpected way. Tabloid coverage of Labour's "loony left" was at a peak and attention alighted on the LCGR fringe meeting at Blackpool Conference in 1982. Despite having happened in previous years, this meeting suddenly attracted enormous and virulently hostile press coverage, with a particularly vicious article in the *News of the World*.

The result was probably not what the editors had expected. Out of interest and chiefly out of solidarity, no fewer than 200 people turned up to the meeting chaired by John Shiers, and Tony Benn, who had not been scheduled to speak, cancelled another engagement to come and give his support. Among the other speakers at this unexpectedly important meeting were Joan Lestor MP, Peter Tatchell, Jo Richardson MP, and Greater London Council leader Ken Livingstone. The last made a rousing call to keep on pressing forward in the Party, to tackle the internal resistance. In this he was echoing the first speech, from Joan Lestor, who reported the serious opposition there was to *The Rights of Gay Men and Women* within the party leadership, and how hard it had been to secure a majority even for supporting an age of consent of 18. (Speeches transcribed in *Gay Socialist – Special Issue: Blackpool Report 1982*). Her warning should have reminded campaigners of just how much work would have to be done, and the difficulty caused by the age of consent would return to haunt Labour several times in the years ahead.

Winning the Conference 1984-5

LCGR decided, therefore, to go for formally winning conference policy in order (it was naively thought) to compel Labour to adopt an equality policy. As anyone who has been involved in trying to have a debate at the Party conference knows, simply getting onto the agenda can be a remarkable achievement in itself – especially if the cause is a minority one, and those most likely to support it are also, simultaneously, being enlisted to support debates on other important subjects. So the first attempt to get onto the agenda (for the 1984 Blackpool conference) was a failure. The second, however, would bring victory at Bournemouth in 1985.

The work put into winning Labour Party policy for the first time was immense, and duly succeeded in persuading ten constituency parties to send in motions based on a carefully-worded LCLGR model, along with a good contingent of LCLGR members as delegates to make sure that the composited motion that came out of it was strong and without ambiguity. On Friday October 4, 1985, Sarah Roelofs, the delegate from Hornsey and Wood Green CLP, moved the first-ever motion at Labour Conference on lesbian and gay rights. It called for an equal age of consent, the end to all discriminatory laws, outlawing of discrimination at work and wherever it occurred, including in child custody cases. It also called for a working party to flesh out the basic policy. The National Executive Committee had recommended that it be remitted, in an effort to avoid being seen to take a decision in particular on the age of consent, but LCLGR was confident of the vote, and was proved right. The debate was televised live, and commentators expressed surprise that the movers had demanded to have a card vote, as they believed they could not win the union votes. The result was a majority of more than 600,000 with a 58% vote in favour. It was, said the London community paper *Capital Gay*, "the greatest single step for Lesbian and Gay liberation" since our movement emerged in 1970.

How did it happen? The answer to this question explains how and why the labour movement had taken up the issue, while also pointing the way ahead. The key votes were, of course, those of the unions, and LCLGR had devoted much energy to securing union support during the week of the conference, but also during the previous period. The solid advances already being recorded in unions were now also paying dividends in the political arena. In fact, the vote at Bournemouth was not the first labour movement policy vote for lesbian and gay equality, but the second: the TUC, meeting the month before, had beaten the Party to it. A motion at Congress moved by NAPO (the National Association of Probation Officers) focussed on discrimination at work, and called for equality legislation to outlaw it, including on pensions policy. NALGO (the local government officers' union) had seconded the motion and it had been carried with one speaker against. From now on, the central body of the British trade union movement had policy on lesbian and gay rights, and the impact of that vote was also felt at the Labour Party conference a few weeks later.

Trade union support was not only a response to the lobbying of lesbian and gay trade unionists. For a terrible twelve months (1984-5) the National Union of Mineworkers had been fighting, in the end, its losing battle against pit closures and job losses. It was faced by the ruthless determination of Thatcher to smash the union that had already thwarted her once before, and had brought down her predecessor, with the full weight of the state. On the side of the NUM had arisen a mass movement of grass roots support – including hundreds of lesbians and gay men working through lesbian and gay support groups. The practical solidarity had not gone unnoticed, lesbians and gays had been welcomed into mining communities, and the NUM had rewarded their commitment with their public thanks, and their votes at the following TUC and Labour conferences. Solidarity is a two-way street, it might be observed, and the already deepening union backing for lesbian and gay equality was powerfully reinforced by the experience of the miners' strike. As Sarah Roelofs stated in the speech moving the motion (printed in *Lesbian and Gay Socialist*, winter 1985):

> ...my former Labour MP (said)... "We should be building the new Jerusalem, not Sodom and Gomorrah". Well, we want no part of your Jerusalem unless it explicitly includes us. The miners' strike showed what we need in practice and a sister from the South Wales mining community said to us this week: "We are your

friends now, and you are our friends, and you have changed our world"...

The majority was not of the order to require the Party to consider the policy for its next manifesto, however, and the opposition of the majority of the NEC meant that nothing could be taken for granted. So there was no debate in LCLGR that it was necessary to build on the 1985 triumph by going back to the following conference and seeking the necessary two-thirds majority. The now experienced conference campaign working party went back to work, and another motion was drafted for Blackpool 1986. The preparation was again professional, and effective, and a composited motion duly appeared on the agenda reaffirming the policy and calling for a manifesto commitment to legislation for lesbian and gay equality. Chris Smith MP spoke strongly in support from the floor. No one spoke against, the NEC, in light of the 1985 vote, had little choice but to support, and a massive 79% vote in favour resulted with only the right wing-led engineers' and electricians' unions voting against among the trade unions. Jo Richardson spoke on behalf of the NEC and declared to conference that "there is no socialism without lesbian and gay liberation." The practical consequence was a one-line reference to outlawing discrimination in the manifesto on which Labour contested the 1987 election, but any disappointment at this was offset by the fact of having made it into a Labour manifesto: another historic first. It was, of course, all rendered rather irrelevant by Thatcher's convincing third victory at the polls.

Meanwhile, following through the focus on winning legislation, LCLGR had also begun to work with CHE and the NCCL to prepare a new draft lesbian and gay rights bill, in the expectation that the next Labour government could now be relied upon to introduce it. The draft was announced at the LCLGR fringe at the Blackpool conference. A conference was organised to discuss it (May 1987), and leading labour movement figures including Ken Livingstone, now MP for Brent East, spoke. Livingstone promised a Labour government would deliver, if elected. Unfortunately, the rest of that event was a disappointing failure, wrecked by in-fighting, and no draft was agreed. The election result made it redundant anyway, but another longer-term consequence was that the original plan to have Labour introduce a single, comprehensive bill rather fell off the campaign agenda. Already, the non-stop anti-gay smear campaigns of the tabloid press had begun to focus on a new target, and once again the community was faced with having to defend rather than to move forward.

Section 28

The right then turned its focus on a new enemy: Labour-controlled local authorities that were considering how to deal with heterosexism in their education policies, on the pressing of local lesbian and gay activists. It all seemed quite reasonable: anti-gay ideas were introduced at an early age, and dealing with them necessarily involved looking at how schools dealt with the subject of families, sex and relationships. To those to whom homosexuality was a corrupting influence on innocent youth, of course, this was more dangerous than anything previously suggested, and to the tabloids it was manna from heaven. Shock horror headlines duly followed, followed by questions in Parliament. Before long, the 1987 Local Government bill had been amended with a new clause: numbered 28, banning local authorities from promoting homosexuality as a pretended family relationship. The supporting speeches were indistinguishable from those that had opposed every proposal on law reform since the days of Wolfenden, but they had the overwhelming support of Tory MPs.

The response from the community is well remembered. The new clause was nothing less than legalised bigotry – a "pink triangle clause" in the words of the message sent by Labour leader Neil Kinnock to the next Pride - and the movement was now confident enough not to take it lightly. The largest-ever protest marches took place, organising tens of thousands of lesbians, gays and bisexuals and their straight supporters, numerous celebrities, MPs and councillors, in meetings, marches, pickets, and lobbies in every town and city in the country. Lesbians took the lead on direct action, with an abseiling descent into the House of Lords during one debate, and the invasion of a BBC news broadcast. Trade unions and Labour Parties condemned the section outright.

However, when the clause was first introduced, Labour's front bench had wavered, and had not opposed it. There was a swift, and successful protest that served to remind shadow ministers of the party's policy, and LCLGR prepared once again to tread the conference road, to make sure it stuck this time. At the 1988 Blackpool conference the third debate on lesbian and gay equality took place around a motion written by LCLGR that reaffirmed existing policies and called not only for the immediate repeal of section 28, but urged local authorities to continue to promote equality. Backed by a unstoppable tide of anger at section 28 and the initial front bench response, it secured 84% this time, winning even more unions to back the vote than before. The leaders of the T&GWU and of the GMW (today's GMB), Ron Todd and John Edmonds, both stated clearly their unequivocal support. Edmonds went on to say, in a message to the fainthearted in the Party,

> You can't cut people out of fair and equal treatment simply because you think some people in the electorate are too prejudiced to support you if you take a just line.

The fringe meeting of 150 was addressed by high level speakers including Robin Cook, Joan Ruddock and Bernie Grant. Cook, a senior member of the shadow cabinet, and long a supporter of equality, called on Labour councils to ignore the section. The press coverage was predictable, however: "Poofters in vote victory" was the headline in the *Daily Star*. (Quotes from the report in *Lesbian and Gay Socialist*, 16, winter 1988).

The bill was finally enacted, and no prosecutions ever took place. As many had feared, it worked without ever being called upon, as cautious councils abandoned any activity that *might* infringe section 28. The mass campaign also withered quickly away, leaving a short-lived lesbian and gay coalition in the form of OLGA, while Stonewall was soon after created as a professional and politically neutral lobby group, unencumbered with the burden of members or democracy.

Labour after Section 28: more conference campaigns

The initial failure of shadow ministers to oppose S28 had done the Labour Party a great deal of damage in a community that was now politicised, but if anyone thought that once this had been put right (as it quickly had been) the problems were over for good, they were in for another shock. In the aftermath of yet another election defeat, the Party decided to undertake a review of policies. In May 1989, deputy leader Roy Hattersley proposed to the National Executive Committee the exclusion of the commitment to an equal age of consent and the repeal of all discriminatory laws from the review, and carried it by a majority. This shocking decision obliged LCLGR once again to run a major campaign, culminating in another conference card vote victory in Brighton, on a motion that spelt out explicitly the previous policy on both issues. Hundreds of delegates wore the special sticker produced to show support, and members across the whole party backed the campaign. The NEC retreat - even worse considering it had actually backed the 1986 and 1988 motions - was overturned by 3.7 to 2.3 million votes.

Just how many conference votes does it require to secure a clear policy? Even now, after four of them, it took a while to resolve this question, and there had to be vigorous lobbying by LCLGR, by newly-established Stonewall, and by Chris Smith and other MPs, to ensure the conference decision was carried out. In the end, it was, and Labour's publication *Opportunity Britain* contained a full paragraph committing a Labour government to the broad outlines of the policy, although on the age of consent it was to a free vote only. Chris Smith wrote that support for LGB equality was now widespread across the party far beyond the committed few, including the front bench (*LCLGR Newsletter no. 4*, summer 1991). The 1992 election was eagerly awaited, expectations being high that at last the Tories could be ousted.

Meanwhile, in the unions, a Lesbian and Gay Trade Union Confederation of activists had been set up, which had met with the TUC, and the latter now published a pamphlet listing unions with policies and structures showing how much progress had now been achieved. This was all taking place while an increasingly desperate Conservative Party embarked on a major offensive on the family, judging this to be a weak point in Labour's challenge, although this time it was single parents rather than lesbians and gays who were blamed for the breakdown of society.

Age of Consent revisited: round one

Early in 1994, through amendments to a criminal justice bill on the age of consent, equality at 16 was lost by just 27 votes, and 18 was passed. John Major and Michael Howard had both come out for this rather than equality, which secured most of the Tory vote. The Labour front bench had supported 16 but had left it to a free vote. Most Labour MPs backed equality, but not all. So despite a long lobbying campaign (in which Stonewall had played a leading part) the criminal law remained discriminatory.

Alarmed by the failure of some Labour MPs to vote for party policy, and even more concerned to make sure of the Party's response to the Tory attack on the issue of the family, LCLGR had already decided to focus on this. It had been the theme of its fringe at the 1993 conference. Shadow Home Secretary Tony Blair spoke there of his opposition to all discrimination and his support for 16, but he affirmed his belief in the two-person heterosexual family as the best option. There followed a fifth conference campaign for Blackpool 1994, of which the chief focus was an explicit call to recognise the equal validity of same-sex relationships with heterosexual in the family debate. The leadership got involved and used the vehicle of its loyal acolytes in Labour Students to replace LCLGR's preferred composite with a much vaguer one. Moving the motion, Katie Hanson from Woking CLP focussed exclusively on the family issue, a theme taken up as well by Peter Purton (Ealing Southall). The seconder, Stephen Twigg (Islington North), dealt with the age of consent. LCLGR knew it would win, but even so there was amazement when the motion obtained 97.6% of the vote. David Blunkett, who as chair had to read out the result, and who had voted for 18, was heard to say "point taken". But the leadership got their way too: vital though the age of consent decision was, all the press reporting was about it rather than the now even more contentious issues of same-sex families, children, and other areas the Tories had focussed on. (LCLGR *Newsletter* 15, autumn 1994).

7. Labour in Government, 1997 to the present

By the time Tony Blair became Prime Minister in 1997 with a crushing majority, the whole labour movement had been won over to a position of supporting lesbian, gay and bisexual equality. The Party's policy had been secured through five conference debates and numerous meetings with party officials, shadow ministers and spokespeople, but chiefly through the taking of the message out to the whole party so that there could be no doubt as to where Labour stood. The unions had witnessed a parallel process, with internal battles to achieve LGB policies and structures increasingly successful. In 1998 the TUC, following a motion carried at Congress the year before, organised the first of what has become its annual LGBT conference, with the right to send a motion to TUC Congress. There is a seat for a LGBT representative on the TUC General Council.

There was (and is) an important overlap between LGBT activists in the unions who were now able to win direct TUC support for campaigns, and those working with the Labour Party. LCLGR had already compiled its *Manifesto for Lesbian and Gay Equality*, launched with the support of UNISON in 1995, which spelt out the agenda for legal change. Its terms now became the list of demands placed on Labour ministers.

For the first time, the community had a party in Government with comprehensive policy on equality, and a Prime Minister who had made a public commitment to it. There were proud, "out" MPs and Chris Smith became the first out gay Cabinet Minister; the *Sun* even identified a "gay mafia" in the cabinet. The whole outlook was transformed, optimism was everywhere. But moving from policy to action proved yet again not to be straightforward. Future historians will have to uncover where exactly the obstacles inside Government were. The obstacles outside were clear enough. They sat in the House of Lords, led some of the religious organisations, and they occupied the editors' chairs in the tabloid press. Despite New Labour's enormous parliamentary majority, there were also voices inside Government that for whatever reasons were not keen on moving the agenda forward. Were they terrified of the expected media onslaught, unwilling to defend their policies? Labour leaders had given an early commitment to equalise the age of consent and to repeal section 28.

Both proved to be rather harder work than originally anticipated.

Age of consent: round two

The first Queen's Speech made no mention of s28, but the new Crime and Disorder Bill offered a vehicle to change the gay male age of consent to 16. The opportunity to remove discrimination from the criminal law altogether was not taken even though the continued misery caused by these laws was highlighted by the successful prosecution of gay men in the case of the "Bolton 7" (March 1998), for breaking the 1967 Act provisions on privacy. The Commons duly passed "16" with a very large majority in June 1998, and ministers promised to tackle the rest of the criminal law agenda in a future promised criminal law review.

Joy at the partial victory was short-lived. The Lords threw it out, and the Government decided to accept this in order not to lose the rest of their Bill. But ministers did promise to reintroduce it as a free-standing measure in the next session. This promise was carried out, and again a large majority supported it in the Commons. Stonewall in particular carried out vigorous lobbying of the Lords to prevent a recurrence of the previous events: but failed. The voices, and the votes, of reaction, were well-organised and loud, vigorously led by die-hard and irreconcilable bigots such as Baroness Young, previously Thatcher's Tory Leader in the Lords, and they won again (spring 1999), rehearsing the same arguments as had been presented every time the subject had been raised since the first debate in 1954. This time, though, Government did not retreat, and instead invoked the rarely-used procedure of the Parliament Act, allowing the Commons to overrule the Lords in certain circumstances. It was a triumphant end to more than thirty years of legal discrimination in which all the arguments about homosexual equality were widely aired.

Armed Forces

Alongside these high-profile debates, the European Court of Human Rights had become involved in British law, not for the first time. They found the UK in breach of the Human Rights convention for outlawing homosexuality in the armed forces (September 1999). The long legal battle run by Stonewall was victorious. But campaigners had to ask, why did the Ministry of Defence continue to defend the case to the last, when it could have conceded it was wrong (not to mention in defiance of Labour's own policy) when Labour took office?

Section 28

The struggle to remove s28 proved no less of a challenge than equalising the age of consent. As with "16", the debate raised the issue of young people and therefore immediately demanded that a view be expressed on whether being lesbian or gay was to be treated as "normal" and equally valid. No amount of hedging would get around the question, as it was posed directly by the opposition, who thought the answer should be "no". To defeat them required that politicians refuted the reactionary position, but despite all the years of work to win acceptance of lesbian and gay *equality*, ministers still tried to appease the defenders of s28 with promises of safeguards for what was taught in sex education. That s28 actually had nothing to do with schools anyway was completely lost in the battle that raged back and forth.

The first step was taken in now-devolved Scotland, despite a massive hostile publicity campaign. The Labour majority, working with other parties in the Scottish parliament, stood firm, and s28 was soon gone north of the border. But they didn't have a House of Lords in Scotland, and the same debates as were heard repeatedly over "16" were run and run again in Westminster. On 24 July 2000, Baroness Young's coalition again rejected repeal. Since the Government had chosen, to the dismay of campaigners, to introduce the proposal in the Lords rather than the Commons, there was nowhere else to go. And with another general election called for spring 2001, no chance to try again. At least Labour's convincing victory in that election meant that there was time to continue with the agenda for equality. Viewed with hindsight, the New Labour government had not achieved much for LGB equality of its own making in its first term. That is not to diminish the importance of the age of consent, the battle around which had achieved an iconic status, especially for gay men in the community. But it was noted that many of the other improvements had come about through court rulings rather than government action, such as that recognising same-sex partners in tenancy succession, and some that were actually made against the government (armed forces).

In fact, it would be 2003, with the House of Lords by then partially reformed, and with the removal of some at least of the completely unaccountable backwoods element, before repeal of s28 finally came about. During that year, too, the remaining discriminatory provisions of the criminal law were removed, and soon after, equal rights to adopt were legislated. By then, LCLGR had taken another major step to securing recognition inside the Labour Party by eventually securing affiliation as a Socialist Society (2002), allowing it to send its own delegate to Conference. Simon Wright was the first LCLGR delegate to address the following Conference. Affiliation also brought access to other channels of communication, such as the National Policy Forum.

Employment rights

Meanwhile, the seeds of the other most significant developments of the second term had already been sown. A trade union member, Lisa Grant, had taken a case against South West Trains for same-sex discrimination in Europe. The European Union had begun the process of requiring member states to outlaw all discrimination in employment in the Amsterdam treaty in 1998, and from 2000 the UK government was thinking about implementation of the ensuing EU Directive. With the achievement of the age of consent and clear commitments from ministers on the rest of the criminal law agenda and on s28, a coalition of labour movement and other LGB campaign groups had been running a powerful lobby for effective anti-discrimination legislation.

One of the first acts of the TUC's new LGBT structure had been a conference in May 1999, actively engaging the unions with Stonewall, LCLGR and other community groups, to launch the campaign. A TUC survey showing the continued extent of discrimination in employment was published (*Straight Up!*, 2001) and ministers and MPs were vigorously pressed to back it. Initially, ministers' response to the pressure had been to promise only a voluntary code of practice. Campaigners knew that this would be next to useless, and a continued reflection of inequality. Compelled anyway by the EU decision, Government changed its mind, and introduced secondary legislation to prevent discrimination in employment and training on grounds of sexual orientation and religion or belief (December 2003). At last, more than two decades after the *Saunders* case, a Labour government had finally outlawed discrimination at work, and another significant part of the equality agenda had been secured.

However, it seemed that Government was determined that when it gave equality with one hand, it would offer comfort to the reactionary brigade with the other. The Employment Equality (Sexual

Orientation) Regulations contained exemptions for the purposes of organised religion, and for benefits conditional on marital status. In other words, religious groups could discriminate, and employers who already gave particular rights to married couples could continue to exclude lesbians and gay men, with particular impact on pensions' survivor benefits. The trade unions rose in revolt on these issues. Seven national unions, co-ordinated by the TUC, challenged the Government in the High Court over the exemptions. The cases failed, but the judge's ruling confined the first exemption to ministers of religion, while the Government promised that it meant to deal with the pensions issue in forthcoming Civil Partnership legislation. Just consider this: it was not usual for unions to challenge a Labour government in the courts anyway, but to do so over an issue of lesbian and gay rights was extraordinary testament to the embedding of equality into unions' concerns.

Pension rights

Getting pensions into the Civil Partnership Bill that was then in Parliament (see below) proved problematic and required further lobbying and campaigning by LCLGR, Stonewall and the unions. It so happened that the Government agreed to include provisions providing equality in pension provision for registered same-sex partners shortly before the unions' appeal against the High Court decision against their challenge was due to be heard, whereupon the case was dropped. Pension entitlement for same-sex partners was equalised with widowers' pension rights. Another significant victory was thus obtained, and once again it could be seen that although only a Labour government could have introduced it, it still had to be compelled to do so by a vigorous, timely and well-organised combined campaign across the labour movement.

Goods and services

In 2005, the Government decided to extend the religion and belief regulations to include protection against discrimination in goods and services, using its existing Equality Bill as the vehicle. The bill was suspended for the election, at which Labour recorded its historic third term, then reintroduced immediately afterwards. The TUC at once called on Labour to extend the same protection to grounds of sexuality. Ministers claimed it was too difficult, but would be done in a future single equality bill. Not satisfied, once again the now well-established alliance rolled into action. LCLGR organised a motion for the 2005 Labour conference. Following a sharp campaign led by Alon Or-bach and Katie Hanson, an unprecedented number of constituency parties (nearly 30) backed the motion and ensured that it got prioritised for debate. Stonewall organised and lobbied behind the scenes in support of an amendment to achieve the desired result to be moved by Lord Waheed Alli in the Lords. The TUC met ministers, briefed MPs and peers, and affiliated unions prepared to support the conference motion. Despite pressure not to force Government's hands by pushing the motion to a vote, LCLGR stood firm and the conference motion, proposed by LCLGR delegate Jo Salmon, was won - the sixth conference victory. This time, and unlike on previous occasions, the policy was swiftly turned into real action. Ministers agreed to prepare appropriate regulations to come into force in October 2006. At the time of writing, there is another argument over potential exemptions from them for religious organisations.

Civil Partnership

Among the equality measures legislated by the Labour government, the Civil Partnership Act that came into force in December 2005 may come to be seen as epoch-making. Same-sex couples could now achieve equal status with married couples in all areas. It was inconceivable that such a measure could have been introduced in the 1980s, for example, and impossible that a Labour government of that time (had they won an election) would have even considered it. Yet in 2004, the bill passed easily with overwhelming (and cross-party) support, and with scarcely notice, let alone a whimper, from the press, despite appearing still further to undermine the "traditional family" that had proved such a fierce battleground on all previous occasions. Such was the effect of a profound social change that has taken place in Britain in the last decade. No "poofters in vote victory" headlines this time, instead pages of friendly coverage of Elton John's civil partnership registration. What a difference 17 years can make. Labour in office had – largely – delivered. It had taken a dedicated, committed and long-term campaign by a relatively small number of activists, but the alliance that had been made with the organised labour movement proved decisive time and again. In the process, the political climate itself had altered beyond recognition.

8. In conclusion (or rather, not....)

Does this mean the battle is over? Certainly not. For a start, initially, sometimes well-intended but clumsy steps towards recognising and including the diversity of the movement itself are far from complete. Most recently, the inclusion of trans people and their urgent concerns in the broader agenda represents unfinished business. Again, there has been welcome Government action (the Gender Recognition Act) that deals with some, but not all, of the issues raised by this community.

More profoundly, it must be remembered that there has been legal protection against sex and race discrimination for thirty years, and every year sees new examples of the deep-rooted sexism and racism that remains. Clearly, this is because they are rooted in society. Challenging the similar depths of prejudice and oppression that face LGBT people today is going to be a long process too. How to start? The alliance already built up that has, at last, secured the legal agenda, will have to be maintained: that is, LGBT campaigners working closely with the labour movement, and in particular, as recent history has so clearly illustrated, deepening their links with the trade union movement. Under the impact of this powerful combination, all parts of the labour movement have been won to the equality agenda. Through continued effort, greater inclusion can be achieved. The government has a big part too, in designing inclusive policies across the whole agenda, and being unequivocal in deliberately promoting LGBT equality. The 2006 review of equality offers the opportunity to continue this task, while the single equality act (expected in 2007) is a chance to level up all the existing protection and plug the remaining gaps.

But it is much easier to change laws than to change society, although the one must act as the necessary condition for the other. Already, at least superficially, there has been a tremendous swing in social attitudes, leaving the opponents of equality increasingly isolated. It would be unwise to assume that they cannot ever make a comeback, in different circumstances. That is why campaigners must continue to work together for a bolder, higher, vision than the words of statutes on their own can offer. Edward Carpenter was groundbreaking in advocating the connection between women's and lesbian and gay liberation and the creation of a socialist society. The words of a train driver from Guildford, who met Carpenter there to discuss industrial issues towards the end of his life, might serve as a suitable conclusion. Edward Carpenter, he said, writing in 1931,

> ... looked with regret upon the leaders of the Labour Movement of today, who with the attainment of power had given up their earlier socialist outlook and were bowing and conforming to the old traditions, empty ceremonies and smug respectability of Society that they formerly fought. (W J Godfrey, in Beith, Edward Carpenter: in appreciation, 94).

The challenge posed by Edward Carpenter, the forgotten pioneer who deserves to be restored to recognition of his honourable place in the history of lgbt liberation, remains uncompleted today, and today's campaigners have a much stronger platform than he had to build on. That platform has been achieved through an alliance of the lesbian and gay rights movement with the labour movement that Carpenter could only dream of. Now the challenge is to finish the job.

9. Sources and further reading

a) Edward Carpenter.
The only text in print is *Homogenic love, and its place in a free society*, extracts in C White, (ed.), *Nineteenth Century writings on homosexuality. A sourcebook*, Routledge, London/New York, 1999.

Loves Coming of Age, The Intermediate Sex and other writings were published in *Edward Carpenter Selected Writings, volume 1: sex*, introduction by Noël Greig, GMP Publishers, London 1984. This is out of print. It does not include anyway the important text *Women, and her place in a free society*, Labour Press, Manchester, 1894.

The other Carpenter texts quoted are available only from libraries. G Beith, (ed.), *Edward Carpenter: in appreciation*, Allen and Unwin, London, 1931, collects some very useful short essays that fill in gaps left in Carpenter's own autobiography, *My Days and Dreams*, Allen and Unwin, London, 1916 (the 3rd ed., 1918 is cited here).

b) Carpenter and the early labour movement
G Elton, *England Arise! A study of the pioneering days of the Labour Movement*, Cape, London/New York, 1931, offers more information than most of the histories of that time.

c) The Labour Party
There are many books describing the creation of the Labour Party. The standard is H Pelling, *Origins of the Labour Party*, Oxford University Press, 2nd ed., reprinted 1979; also see A Thorpe, *A History of the British Labour Party*, Macmillan, London, 1997.

d) Lesbian and Gay Rights
The parliamentary battle (to 1990) is thoroughly described by Stephen Jeffrey-Poulter, *Peers, Queers and Commons. The struggle for Gay Law Reform from 1950 to the present*, Routledge, London/New York, 1991. Graham Robb, *Strangers, Homosexual Love*

in the Nineteenth Century, Picador, London 2003, is a splendid and thoroughly researched account of the reality of life in Victorian Britain. There were several accounts written by participants in the British lesbian and gay movement during the '80s, covering general experiences as well as particular (e.g. Peter Tatchell on Bermondsey), and numerous pamphlets and booklets, few of which are now available. These are cited as they appear.

e) Other sources consulted
Various Labour Party official programmes and pamphlets (as cited in the text - published by the Labour Party or the Independent Labour Party), the NEC discussion paper *The Rights of Gay Men and Women* (1981), the TUC's annual Congress reports, the Minutes of the TUC General Council of 29 August 1924, and the article by Herbert Tracey in *Labour Magazine*, October 1924, both courtesy of the TUC Library. For the campaigns of the 1980s and after, use has been made of LCLGR's quarterly journal *Lesbian and Gay Socialist*, and its replacement from 1990, LCLGR Newsletter, articles from *Capital Gay and Gay Times*, etc: but chiefly from the writer's memory as a participant.

Notes

1 Henry Hyndman (1842-1921), was born into a wealthy, Tory family, and converted to socialism.

2 William Morris (1834-96), writer, artist and socialist.

3 Tom Mann (1856-1941), trade union militant and joint founder of the Transport and General Workers Union in 1897; Ben Tillett (1860-1943), leader of the "New Unionism" following the 1889 dock strike, Labour MP 1918-31; Will Thorne (1857-1946), helped found the Gas Workers' Union (a forerunner of today's GMB); Labour MP 1906-45.

4 Annie Besant (1847-1933), early advocate of birth control, key supporter of the 1888 match girls' strike, supporter of women's suffrage, Indian home rule and many progressive causes.

5 Peter Kropotkin (1842-1921), Russian anarchist and writer.

6 Havelock Ellis (1859-1939), champion of women's equality and sex education, author of the seven volume *Studies in the Psychology of Sex*, wrote *Sexual Inversion* (1896); Olive Schreiner (1855-1920), South African writer, opponent of racism, advocate of women's liberation; Henry Salt (1851-1939), humanitarian and social reformer, advocate of vegetarianism.

7 In the *Terminal Note* to *Maurice*.

8 Henry Labouchère (1831-1912), a Liberal MP who never secured political advancement.

9 Richard Butler MP (1902-1982), minister for education in Churchill's government, home secretary 1963-5.

10 Kenneth Robinson MP (1911-1996) became minister for health in Wilson's 1964 government and was the first chair of mental health charity MIND.

11 This is why this pamphlet, in using "lesbian and gay" for most of the text, is reflecting the actual language, and concerns, of those engaged in the struggles of those times. The TUC incorporated trans issues into its (then) LGB structure in 2002, and LCLGR did the same in 2004.